Writing a Business Plan That Works

Create a Winning Business Plan and Strategy for your Start-up.

Table of Contents

Chapter 1: Who needs a business plan?

Budding entrepreneurs are all around. They can come from any walk of life and can rise to the heights of business success. For every success story there are countless stories of those who have tried and failed. There are also many entrepreneurs who have made a small scale success of their business, maybe not wishing to take it further or possibly unable to navigate the business to the next level.

It will probably be obvious to anyone starting in business that they will need a business plan. If nothing else this plan will be required by the banks or finance houses to approve the start up funds. Often this is all a business plan is considered necessary for but in fact it should play a far more important role in any business.

Like anything in life, planning makes the job in hand easier. A business plan allows you to set targets and goals, monetary or otherwise. It forces you to consider what you can reasonably achieve in a certain time period. It can also be very beneficial in ensuring your ultimate goal is broken down into manageable chunks.

In reality a business plan is essential for any business which wants to succeed. Whether you are a start up or a long established company, without a target to aim for you will lose drive and initiative. If a business does not know where it is going it is highly likely to flounder and at the least stagnate. In all probability it will fail. This is true for anything in life, without a vision of the future you will sway between decisions and be unable to choose the best path.

Many smaller companies or start ups will probably have these targets and goals firmly established in their heads, after all how many people want their new business to fail? The issue with this is that these ideas are not necessarily communicated to the others involved with the business and they consequently lack drive and direction. A secondary issue, which everyone hopes would not happen, would be if you, the business founder have an accident and are unable to contribute to the business for a period of time. The remaining staff would make decisions on what they felt was best for the business, possibly pulling it in multiple directions in the process.

Most importantly, starting a business and having a goal to succeed is not enough. In order to succeed there will need to be many mini-goals, each one contributing to the overall success of the business. These mini-goals need to be recorded along with the strategy that will be adopted to get the business where it needs to be.

A business plan is not just written to establish the goals of a business; the plan is also useful to see where the business has been. Whether in good times or bad it can be a useful tool to look at the goals previously set, how they were achieved and how they affected the business in terms of growth and security. Studying this information can lead to interesting data which will assist in deciding where the business goes next and how it does it. Hind sight is always a wonderful thing and in these situations can be usefully utilised to ensure the business goes in the direction you want it to.

The plan will also allow you to make quick decisions when needed should your market or business needs change. Knowing where you are going and how you intend to achieve it will make it far simpler to adjust your business to the latest changes in an increasingly demanding environment.

Finally, a business plan is an excellent way to show other companies that you are serious about what you are doing. By taking the time to draw up the plan you are recognising the importance of planning. With a plan success is not just possible it is almost a given. Others that know you have a plan will see you are a force to be reckoned with and treat you with a professional courtesy.

Chapter 2: What is a Business Plan?

Having read chapter one you will understand that a plan is made up of goals and an ultimate target. You should now be aware of why every business should have one. But what exactly is it?

A business plan is a document drawn up by the owner (s) of a company. This could be one individual about to start a business or it can be a huge conglomerate with many shareholders, a board and a chairman of the board. In the case of the shareholder owned companies it would be the board who would decide the best plan for the business. The document can be a few pages long or can be made up of a multitude of pages. The length is down to the amount of detail that is required in the plan.

The plan is a summary of the facts and figures available and must be accurate. In the case of start ups this plan will be needed to encourage financiers to back the plan. If they should check or require proof of the facts given you must be able to provide it, hence why the plan should be accurate. The plan is slightly different if you are a start up compared to an ongoing concern:

Start Ups

The plan will need to summarise your current financial situation. The amount of funds available must be shown and the resources which need to be purchased. There should be an analysis of your target market and the reasoning for why your product or service is needed and will be viable. Most importantly the plan needs to be realistic as to how much income can be expected as you build the business. All these facts will allow you to put together a cash flow forecast. This document will show your starting cash, realistic income and potential expenses over a period of the first year. The end of this document will provide a figure which, if negative, will show the amount of additional funds you need to get your new business through the all important first year. It is important to allow for unexpected additional expenditure.

Ongoing Concerns

The needs of a currently operating business will be slightly different. The plan will be based entirely on fact. The cash flow forecast can be linked to two or three years worth of profit and loss which will then provide realistic projection figures for the coming year, it may even be worth extending the forecast to two years. As a company already trading the market has already been shown to be viable. The emphasis in this plan is to show what will be needed in terms of capital to enable the company to reach its next goal.

A business plan is more than just a set of financial statements. It is a document which maps out the journey so far. This journey could be the process by which a start up has been deemed necessary or it could be the story of how the company has successfully traded for this long. It also maps out the destination. This is split into what is achievable in the short term – usually one to two years, the medium term – usually five years and the long term – the ten year plan.

A business plan is an essential prop in making the daily decisions and the big decisions. With a plan you can assess the need for equipment, personnel and product changes against a backdrop of current markets and the path you are trying to take. Without it a series of good decisions may ultimately lead nowhere.

Chapter 3: Can you write your own business plan?

Any document can be written on your own if required, there is no legal need to have a business plan drawn up by someone with a professional qualification. However, there are pros and cons to writing it on your own.

The plan must look professional, drawn together in a logical order with all the pertinent information analysed and presented in an easy to read manner. A prospective backer may only have five minutes to look at the plan and decide whether it is worth looking at further. It is therefore important to be thorough when drawing up the plan and if you have any doubts to seek professional advice.

Consideration must also be given to the knowledge you have of your business or start up. A professional will make a good looking presentation but may not cover all the points and concerns you wish to. You are, after all, the one who knows the most about your new venture.

Perhaps the best answer is to write your own plan and have a professional available for advice when needed. Just don't forget to include the professional fees in your cash flow!

One additional point that should be raised is that sometimes drawing up a business plan will highlight the fact that this particular business is not actually viable. By drawing up the business plan yourself you will avoid the embarrassment of attempting to finance a project that will not work.

Chapter 4: Key elements of a good business plan.

No matter how good your business ideal is you will never get finance without a good plan, even if you don't need the investment it is unlikely the business will get off the ground unless you know where you are going. As already mentioned every plan is unique but the following elements are essential:

The mission Statement also known as the vision statement

This is the part where you will need to talk about the goals we mentioned in chapter one. The plan needs to be fairly concise. It must be easy to follow and understand for anyone reading it. If the business plan is to assist with obtaining finance it will need to provide enough information for a potential investor to see how you will achieve these goals. The mission statement will need to be very detailed if you are intending to use the plan to assist with gaining finance. If the plan is just for the company to know where they are heading then less detail is needed.

The opening part of this statement should state what it is you are aiming for. This statement should then be split into three sections. The first section covers the short term goal, namely the first year. Start ups will need as much detail as possible in this section and preferably break the year down into monthly goals. This will make it easy for any company member or investor to monitor the progress and see whether the company is where it should be. This detailed breakdown will also allow potential investors or partners to evaluate the business and see potential flaws. By providing succinct, very short term targets it will be possible to adjust a specific target according to economic trends. This also allows targets to be adjusted without disturbing the main goal if you realise that the estimations and predictions the plan is based on have not turned out as expected.

Company & product description

In this section you will need to describe your company. For start ups it is a good idea to explain your reasoning for the name as this is part of the marketing of the company. Existing companies will need to provide a brief history of the company. The history should cover the highs and lows of the company as this will show it has not all been plain sailing; that the business is adaptable and has risen to every challenge. This detail may also highlight a trend in the ups and downs of a company that you had not previously noticed. The company structure should be listed here, not only does this show excellent organisational skills and it provides a reference for those working at the company. This is not the detailed names and positions list. It should be a simple table showing the general hierarchy. Of course if you are a start up it may just be you available initially. In this situation it is important to provide an insight into your workload and when you feel additional help would be both required and affordable.

It is also very important to confirm at which level you are targeting your company – wholesale, retail or industrial. You should show who you intend to sell to and how you intend to distribute the product.

You should cover the detail of what the product or service is and at which part of the market it is aimed. Whilst the description does not need to be too technical it will need to paint a clear picture of what the product does. Pictures may even help in this section particularly if colour is a key factor in your products appearance. The reader should be able to visualise the product. If presenting the plan in person it might be helpful to have the product with you and let the potential investor hold – providing this is possible. If you are offering a service and presenting the plan in person it may be possible to demonstrate the service you are providing.

Why your product or service is unique

This is a useful section regardless of the purpose of the plan. For those seeking investment it is the opportunity to sell the product or service. If the plan is just for company direction it is a chance to remind everyone just how good your product is. It is very important you, and those involved in your company, believe in your product. If you don't then you will never be able to sell it effectively. This section gives you the opportunity to list all the good things about your ideal. Never focus on the negative of other products. You must emphasis all the good characteristics of the product you are offering and keep reminding the reader why this is unique. They have to believe they need this product. It will probably be very helpful if you know someone who is good at selling who can assist with this section.

Market analysis

No business will get far without this. You can have the best product in the world but if there is no market for it your business will be doomed from the start. The starting point needs to show some evidence of market research even if this has been done over the internet. You should show the size of the current target market and the growth it has been experiencing. There should be some informed predictions on how the market will continue to grow.

A review of similar products would be useful and how they fit into the market. This should then automatically lead to the point that there is nothing like your service / product currently available but that there is clearly a gap in the market for it.

This is also the opportunity to show you understand your competition. It is best to show what service your competitors are offering and what they are missing and the fact that you will be offering that missing piece. This could be that one competitor offers the product but not the aftercare or that two companies offer complementary goods but don't support each other. The analysis should also look briefly at what would happen if one of these competitors did change their methods and how it might affect your own business plans. Price should be mentioned in this section. You will need to show whether you will be the same price as your competitors but with better quality products or extras that the competition do not offer. It is important to show you know your market, whether by many years of experience in the given industry or by evidence of having spoken to market experts.

All of these factors will show you have a serious business prospect and have planned for every foreseeable eventuality. This is essential if you wish your plan to be considered by investors.

Management team

As previously mentioned the start up may be just you and no other parties. If this is the case then this section will need to focus on how you foresee the management structure growing. The purpose of this section is to highlight the strengths of the company. Each person involved with have a speciality field; this could be the product or finance or customer support. The structure of this should show each member of the management team as head of one of these departments. It should provide their skills and qualifications and thereby assure a potential investor that all elements of the business are being looked after by professionals who know what they are doing.

To assist in analysing the relevant skills and departments required it will probably be useful to assess the tasks which need completing daily. This does not need to form part of the plan but is a useful exercise. You should be able to organise these tasks into departments, each with a clear line of reporting from operator to senior management. It will then be possible to determine the staff that will be required. Finally you could relate each task to how it will generate revenue or contribute to the company.

Having decided the departments and personnel required you will be able to work out the total number of personnel needed to hit the targets you have set. This process involves calculating what the average employee can achieve in a day compared to how much you would like to achieve to hit your target. For example if an employee can produce 10 products in a day and your target is 100, you will need 10 employees.

Marketing strategy

This is one of the most important areas of the business. Without this the business will never hit any targets and will never be a success. There are many factors to consider which are listed below. It is not necessary to put all this information into the plan but it is advantageous to go through the process and keep a record of the strategy.

You will have already worked out the target market and the size of the market. Now you will need to estimate your market share. There is no hard and fast rule regarding how you calculate this. The variables are considerable. A few important ones are the location of target area, distribution issues, and pricing. In order to estimate your market share as accurately as possible you will need to look at the following two factors.

- Growth of the market. Most industries will grow year upon year and this is an important factor in your calculations. Growth in the market will mean there are more users of your product or service available. Some of these new users can be directed directly at your product.
- Conversions – market users can be split into those who are new to the market, established users and long term users who may be looking to stop purchasing this particular product.

From these figures you should be able to work out an approximate number of people that should convert to your product and whether you are better off targeting new, established or long term users.

Having decided on the size of the market available to you and the approximate type of person you will need to look at how to get them to purchase your product. Every market is different and you will need to decide what will work best in your industry. For some big radio or television advertising campaigns can produce good results. Others may work better using the internet and social media sites and small businesses growing slowly might prefer word of mouth.

A second important part of the marketing strategy is working out where to position your product. Is it at the top end; aimed at prestige customers. Maybe the emphasis needs to be on value for money. To assist in answering this question you will need to look at how your competitors have positioned themselves in the market. If your product is exactly the same as one of your competitors then you will have an idea of where to start. If you have more to offer then you may wish to start at their level to offer better value than they are. Identifying what your product has that others do not allows you to target the market from this angle.

Having now worked out where to position your product and who to target you will need to check that your distribution network is up to the task and that the costs of production will not outweigh the selling price. You will then be ready to look at the promotional side. The promotional side is the most important as it generates sales. A good promotion is all about releasing only the information you want customers to know about. The wording and where to release these advertisements requires serious thought.

There will be multiple calculations and observations with pages of notes involved in working all this out. You will then need to summarise the facts and figures into one concise statement on your plan with one line for each of the following categories:

- Advertising budget
- Packaging – description and trademarks or service marks.
- Publicity strategy – the approach and media which will be used.
- Sales Promotions – sales methods including any promotions you intend to run.
- Personal sales – You will probably need several lines on this one. It should summarise the pricing procedures, the returns policy, how leads will be generated and how sales bids will be presented. It is also good practice to look at salesperson responsibilities, rewards and incentives and the customer service policies.

Your market strategy has now been decided and all the calculations and paperwork can be filed for reference if needed.

Strengths & weaknesses

This section is mainly regarding your product but can be used to assess the market place in general. A business plan should never concern itself with the weaknesses of its competition. This should have been explored when undertaking the viability of the business. Focusing on other issues is not a professional approach and will not win investors.

It is important to be thorough. Identifying why you product is better than the competition will highlight its strengths and will probably be a fairly easy exercise. It will be much more difficult to identify weaknesses with your product but working out if there are any will have some very positive effects. Firstly, identifying a weakness will allow you to take action and improve the product to eliminate the weakness. Secondly showing weaknesses and your intended action on your plan will show to those looking at your plan that you are taking a professional approach to your business and looking at all aspects as fairly as possible.

Cash flow projection

For many people this can be the hardest part of a plan and is essential to gaining credible investors. Most people starting in business will know the industry well, they will understand the products already available and where their product will fit in. They will probably have a good idea of how to market the product and who will be most likely to use it. What they may lack is financial skills and terms like "profit and loss", "cash flows" or "Balance Sheet" will be daunting.

Thankfully you have done much of the work already. The cash flow projection is simply a list of the cash expected to come into your business versus the cash that is expected to go out. It is not an exact document as you cannot expect to know everything that will happen in the coming months. It needs to be as accurate as possible as it will be useful in the day to day running of the business – to guide whether you are staying within the financial parameters set.

A typical cash flow projection would show the coming year with a monthly breakdown and totals. It would appear as follows:

Cash in hand at beginning of the month (or at start up).
Cash in hand at the end of the month

Receipts

Sales
Less returns and allowances
Collections on accounts receivable – this is only applicable if you have credit customers and would not have a figure for the first month of a start up.
Interest and any other income
Funds received from any loans / finance arrangements
Contributions from owner

Total receipts.
Total cash available (Total receipts plus cash on hand at beginning of month)

Expenses

Advertising
Commission and fees
Employee benefits
Insurance
Bank or credit interest
Mortgage Interest
Material supplies
Office expenditure
Any other interest
Other interest expenses
Pension & profit sharing plans
Purchases for resale
Rent or lease for property
Rent or lease for vehicles or equipment
Repairs and maintenance
Sundry receipts.
Taxes and licences
Travel
Utilities
Wages
Utilities
Unforeseen expense

Miscellaneous

Sub total

Principle loan payment
Capital purchases
Other start up costs
 Owners' withdrawal

Total Cash Paid out

Cash on hand at end of month (transfer this figure to the box at the start).

Additional useful info.

Sales Volume
Accounts receivable balance
Bad debt balance
Inventory on hand
Accounts payable balance
Depreciation

This format can be adjusted to suit your individual needs with additional lines being added in if necessary or lines removed. The end result should show all expected income and outgoings month by month. An ongoing total will accumulate to show an expected yearly cash figure. This figure is not the same as your end of year profit. Other calculations are processed to arrive at an end of year profit figure. The cash flow projection will provide you and any investors with information regarding the funds required to ensure the business can survive through the first year.

Revenue projections

When projecting the income for a start up it is highly unlikely that you will be accurate. This should not be considered a problem as the projections are not set in stone and can be adjusted once you have more information. In particular several months of sales may change this projection. An established business can use past year figures to come to a realistic revenue projection. A business just starting up will have to rely on educated estimates. The important part of these projections is that you justify how you came to your figures. It is never good to leave the reader guessing such important data.

Revenue projections should be based on your assessment of the market and your estimated market share. These two figures will have to match if your plan is to be taking seriously. If you are listing them at different values you will need to explain where the difference is.

Whilst there is a valid argument for being conservative with your revenue figures there is no harm in working out the conservative figure and then looking at a slightly more aggressive option. For instance, if you assume you will have no sales people in the first year and that you will release one new product a year for the first five years. You will come up with a very different figure to if you plan to employ two sales people and release three new products to each sector of the market each year for the first five years. The second option may be a little too much, it might be an over ambitious dream. But if you don't think big you will never be big so a little aggression in the figures will help you push a little harder than you may have done.

An additional benefit of this tactic is that investors will see someone who wants to get somewhere. This will assist in your negotiations as no matter how good the business plan is investors need to believe that you will do everything possible to make the business a success and repay the funds borrowed with interest.

Summary

As hard as it may appear the business plan needs to be fairly concise; you don't want to lose potential investors because they floundered in page two's vision of the future. One purpose of the document is to get investors attention and to get them to open their wallets. The second aim is to provide a document that the management can use to understand where the company is going and how it intends to get there.

The summary is there to remind potential investors or company management of the company foundations, its aims, strengths and weaknesses and the route it will take to get where it wants to go. This section of the plan should serve as a quick reminder of the main points of the plan. The summary should highlight the company aims, the projected first year revenue and profit. This is the last bit to be read so should be almost like a sales pitch. Highlighting the best parts of the business plan.

This section should be used to focus the reader on why this company is such a good investment. It should not go into any depth and should be kept fairly short. It is a good chance to remind them that you are offering a new product or service that will literally dominate the market. A reference should be made to remind them of any particularly relevant skills you or someone else in the company has. Anything that persuades an investor that they are making a good business decision will assist in them parting with their funds.

Mentioning personal information in this section will assist the investor in bonding with you and make them more likely to want them to give you the capital needed.

Chapter 5: Example of a business plan

As the title says, the following is an example of a business plan. It is important to remember that there is no right or wrong way to put a plan together, you just have to make sure the pertinent facts are included.

Business Plan

Your Business Name

Address

Address 2

City,

 ZIP Code

Telephone

Fax

E-Mail

Mission Statement

It is usually best to write this last. If you do not you may find you will need to edit it many times!

This statement should be no more than two pages long

Read the guide on this section and visualize the points you would wish to raise in five minute meeting – that is what needs to be included.

This section must convey your enthusiasm for the product It should be professional but concise.

State the purpose of this statement and if you are applying for a loan make sure you mention the exact amount you would like. You should also specify how it will be used and how this will enable your business to be profitable. This means you will be able to repay the loan.

Make sure your short, medium and long term goals are included.

Company & Product Description

It is important to specify whether an existing company or a start up. You must list the legal entity of the company. It could also be useful to mention why you chose this entity.

Include either company history for an established business or reasons for starting the company.

One line can be dedicated to stating what is important to you in business.

Indicate you understand your target industry and whether it has been growing or not.

Describe the product or service you wish to offer, ensure a reader can visualize it and how useful it will be. Highlight what the product does

Unique Product

Specify what is special about your product, particularly in relation to similar products on the market.

Emphasis good points of your product never the negative ones of the competition.

Market Analysis

Research can be done via the internet or your local library. Look at data sources such as industry papers or government statistics.

It may also be helpful to do a little of your own research. Questionnaires can be a good source of feedback.

Be as specific as possible. Use the facts you have. But do restrict it to facts.

Review the products available in your target market and the gap available for your product.

Don't forget the reasons the gap is there and how your product will fill it.

Management Team

Highlight the skills brought to the business by each of the management team. Any professional qualifications should be shown here.

Ensure you include the structure for day to day transactions, who reports to whom?

Make sure the contingency plan is mentioned for if the daily manager is unable to work for any reason.

Show the departmental structure and the key positions. It is also useful to include position descriptions for key employees.

Marketing strategy

You will need to explain the various procedures concerning the following:

- Production techniques and costs

- Quality control

- Customer service

- Inventory control

- Product development

- Location of product and target market

- Requirements of location to allow production. Think about the space, type of building and power required. It may also useful to assess whether large vehicles will need to access your premises.

- You should indicate if your premises need to be near an airport or train station.

Define whether you think the market is growing or not with your reasons.

Define your projected market share and how you came to this figure.

Demonstrate your knowledge of the industry.

It will be worth putting in figures for rent, building maintenance, utilities, insurance and any building improvements you wish to do

You should also consider your business hours and whether you need to be somewhere with passing trade or not.

Dedicate a short paragraph to the number of employees – either employed or will need to be. You should indicate whether they are skilled labor or not. If you have a set pay structure it may be useful to include this.

It is important to mention your stock; if you make this product then you should list what materials are needed to make each product.

An important part of the marketing strategy is the supplier. It is worth logging several suppliers of your product and indicating which one is your first choice.

Also note in this section whether you are planning to allow customers credit? If you are it is worth re-evaluating to ensure you definitely need to offer this service.

For those with credit terms you will need to assess how they will pay and when you will need assistance chasing the debts in.

A standard age debtor's report will look like this:

If you do offer credit, then a debtors report will be printed weekly.	Total	Current	30 Days	60 Days	90 Days	Over 90 Days
Accounts Receivabl e Aging						

There will always be some slow paying customers so the following will need to be decided:

- When do you make a phone call?

- When do you send a letter?

- When do you get your attorney to threaten?

Finally tie in all the above facts to which path you have chosen to use for marketing and the reasons why.

Strengths & Weaknesses

Remember to focus on your product or service, not the competition.

If possible highlight a weakness and then the solution

It is acceptable to relate the strengths to products manufactured by the competition.

Cash flow projections

The Cash flow projection is actually only one of the projections that should be included in this business plan. The breakdown of the cash flow projection has already been shown. Other relevant documents are: a financial plan consisting of a 12-month profit and loss projection, a four-year profit and loss projection (optional), a projected balance sheet, and a break-even calculation.

Together these documents will give a fairly accurate picture of where your company is at and where it should be in twelve months time. Of equal importance is the fact that the process of thinking through the financial plan will improve your knowledge of the inner financial workings of your company.

12-Month Profit and Loss Projection
In some ways this is the most important part of the plan. Nobody starts a business not intending to make a profit. If you piece together all the following information into one sheet you will be able to see at a glance whether you can turn a profit each month and whether there should be a profit at year end.

This is a useful document to keep track of how closely the business is following the plan.

The sales projections can be worked out by creating a sales forecast. You will need to forecast sales, cost of goods sold and expenses for each of the next twelve months. These figures will provide you with a monthly and yearly profit figure.

Any projection of sales or profit should be backed up by a note explaining how you came to your conclusions regarding a realistic sales figure, an accurate cost of goods (in relation to the sales figure) and the expenses you expect to incur.

Whilst the detail of your research does not need to be included in this plan it is advisable to keep a record of the major assumptions made and the research done to back this up. This will be invaluable when presenting the business plan or even when just discussing it with your business partner.

Four-Year Profit Projection (Optional)

This is exactly the same as the 12 month plan but extended over four years. It is not essential or even expected to be included in the business plan but it is sometimes useful.

It will certainly help you with monitoring the businesses progression and will provide a good base record for future decisions to be made on.

Again, any research does not need to be included in the plan but should be safely saved for reference.

Projected Cash Flow

As already mentioned, cash is not the same as profit. Profit indicates a healthy business with a good market demand. Cash shows whether or not the company can afford to pay its bills or staff the next time it needs to.

Cash flow projections are very important for businesses. They assist in working out when payment to the different suppliers can be made and can help with collecting payments in from credit customers.

Revenue Projections

Before any business can commence trading they must work out whether the business is viable and the value of funds needed to be available for the start up. There are a variety of tools available to assist in this. Before any income stream can be estimated we need to work out the expenses in relation to this income. Using percentage based calculations we can take the hoped for income and calculate the cost of sales for it.

There will be many other expenses before you can start to run your business. To ensure you have sufficient capital to cover all the likely expenditures a projection is a fantastic idea.

Like many things in life no matter how careful the planning there is always an unexpected surprise. It makes sense to assume there will be one, particularly in the first year of a new business. The best way to deal with this is to add an additional line in the cash flow projection showing 'contingencies' and put your best estimate in here. It is also possible to add a little too all other sales prices to generate enough funds to cover the unexpected. However, this method will destroy the accuracy of the many prepared budgets.

The best way to decide on a figure to keep back for contingencies is to talk to others in the same field and note how many funds they needed in the first year. It is also good to talk to others who have experience to get a good idea of how much to allow for contingencies. If it really impossible to find someone to assist with this then 20% works well as a general rule.

The expenses on the forecast will need to be explained and if necessary proof of the research shown. The amounts given by your sources should be shown broke down into bite size chunks of data. You should also include any ownership loans; noting how much has been contributed by who and where. Also show how much of the ownership belongs to each person.

You should take each item and look at its cost to work out a minimum value so that you know how much you will need to sell each item for.

If you are aware or become aware of particular items, machinery or assets which will need to be purchased for the business it is a good idea to add then into the forecast as soon as possible. This will help ensure the funds are available when needed.

An often overlooked item is expenditure before the business start up. This can be significant and usually comes out of the owner's or manager's pocket. It is very important to keep a track of these expenses as they will be added into the final figures. They may also be used when looking at repeat expenses for future years.

The cash flow will show if you do not have enough cash at any given time whether it is after one month or one year. If there is clearly a hole in the funds that cannot be resolved by moving payments around then you will need to increase the start-up capital needed. A good cash flow will show you when you need the extra funds.

Again, don't forget to explain any assumptions.

Some expenses may be prepaid, i.e. you pay three months worth of phone bills because you know you will get a better deal. In the cash flow it will show as one payment but in the projection it will show as three individual ones. These need to be looked for and adjusted on the cash flow when possible.

The same can be said for larger purchases, whether a quarterly tax bill or monthly revenue payment. These transactions should be thought about and included in the cash flow as soon as possible

Additional items such as depreciation does not appear on the cash flow so can be ignored as no cash ever leaves the business. However loan payments and equipment purchases do not usually show on the profit and loss but do involve cash leaving the business. This should also be borne in mind.

Opening Day Balance Sheet

Balance sheets can appear baffling to the uninitiated. There are many figures on the top with a total that must agree to the bottom figures. It is one of the most important financial reports for any business.

The balance sheet lists all items on value to a company (not individually). These are known as the assets. It then lists the liabilities – which is anything owed by the company. If you take the liability value away from the asset value you will be left with the value of the business to the owner.

An opening day balance sheet will be fairly simple. The assets will be the initial purchases of machinery and similar whilst the liabilities will be any funds put into the business by you or someone else. It is possible to estimate these figure for the end of the first year trading to show how viable the business is. This can be of particular interest to investors and should be considered.

Break-Even Analysis
It is always useful to know at what stage your business will break even. By knowing this you will automatically know when you will start making a profit. The formula is as follows:

$$\text{Breakeven Sales} \quad = \quad \frac{\text{Fixed Costs}}{1\text{- Variable Costs}}$$

You should know what your fixed costs are after having prepared the financial documents. If you have made any assumptions when calculating these figures, be sure to keep a record of your workings for future reference or to show potential investors. Having this information to hand will ensure a potential investor knows you understand your market and the needs of your business.

Summary

This is the opportunity to review the facts and figures presented.

Reiterate the important information in the plan in bullet form

Remind the reader of what it is you want

Inform them again of why your product is unique and will succeed

Keep it concise with a slight emphasis towards a selling pitch

Chapter 6: Planning a start up strategy

Every business starts with a dream. This probably involves a vision of a future where your product or service is known throughout the world and is associated with quality and value for money. Most people will have had the ideal simmering in their head for some time before taking the first steps. This is particularly true if it is your first business venture. Many of the initial hurdles have been cleared by creating the business plan. You will have conducted market research and confirmed there is a market for your product. The product is viable in terms of cost and the expected retail price. These costs have included an evaluation of the personnel required and the packing and distribution networks needed. The plan will have assisted greatly in obtaining finance to help get you new venture off the ground. But all of this and you have yet to make a single product!

The business plans provides the goals and potentially the motivation if you should falter but now you need a strategy which will ensure your business goes from nothing to a success. This is unlikely to happen overnight but the following points will assist in planning your start up strategy.

Financial assistance

Unless you are either a qualified accountant or very experienced in dealing with numbers, profit and loss, cash flows and even balance sheets you will struggle with keeping the day to day transactions recorded and formatted. Without these figures all your projections will be useless. You need to be able to compare the actual sales, costs and profit to the business plan to see what you are doing right and wrong.

There are two ways of approaching this. Firstly is to hire a bookkeeper for a few hours each week to log all the transactions, reconcile the banks and present the ongoing data. A few hours a week will be enough to start with but as the business grows so will the hours required. Of course, hiring a bookkeeper is an additional expense but it is a time saver. If you are not familiar with these processes it can drain a large amount of time which you could be using for marketing the business. The second option is to undertake a course so that you are better prepared to tackle the record keeping and reports required. The issue with this, of course, is time. Have you the spare time to undertake a course before you start the business? It I unlikely you will want to spare the time while the business is starting up and your time can be better spent elsewhere.

Goals

The business plan will have presented your short term goals as well as medium and long term goals. In order to effectively start the business and maximize your limited time you will now need to create daily or weekly goals. Breaking down the procedures and the processes you will need to do into day by day targets will allow you to focus on small issues and take one step at a time. There can be a lot of work to be done to reach a monthly or quarterly goal and, particularly for a start up, this can become overwhelming. By creating these mini goals you will create detailed daily tasks list which you know do the required job. By understanding these processes you will be able to refine them and adjust them for any issues as you go. The preparation which goes into this will alleviate much of the stress which comes with a business start up. Your focus can be on the job in hand safe in the knowledge that the plan will bring it all together.

Personnel

Your plan has established what personnel you require, including how many and of what caliber. The issue is that even with these factored in to your financial plans you will not have a large amount of funds to attract the best marketing or sales people. It is important to now look at what you are able to offer. Sales people might be happy to take a basic salary and commission depending on the sales they generate. Marketing people might be able to do similar based on the success of their marketing campaigns. But the one thing that everyone should respond to is buying into the vision. If the personnel you hire believe that they are joining a firm which is committed to obtaining a certain market sector or to becoming the best supplier of a certain product then they can see an incentive for joining. Even if the financial reward is not great now they will see it is possibly for these rewards to be significantly greater as the business grows – and they will be instrumental in that growth.

The market

The plan has identified the market and you will even have worked out a plan as to how to approach this market. You should also know which part of the market you are pursuing and how you will pursue it. However, to make this dream a reality you will need the same time and resources as with the financial aspect. The marketing must be broken down into small, achievable daily or weekly tasks. You or the marketing personnel must be able to report on whether those tasks have been achieved. Of equal importance is when they have not been achieved and why. Your business plan should have looked at the best price to sell at and who to target first. The biggest issue with a start up is that you are generally unknown and will need to build your market presence. A fantastic way to boost your presence is to target a company which is dissatisfied with the product they are purchasing – probably because of the service received is poor or the product does not do exactly what they want it to. This is the ideal candidate to pursue and supply. The approach is simply to offer what they need and are missing at the moment. Most importantly make sure you exceed their expectations every time and your reputation will grow. This will ensure you attract additional customers and a larger market share.

Change

Even the best business plan cannot foresee the future. One of the most important elements in any start up or even established business strategy is the ability to change. Your plan is not set in stone; it should not be followed regardless. It is a guide and you must be constantly monitoring your chosen market, your specific customer needs and the economy as a whole. It is important never to be afraid to change tact and respond to the developing need of your customers. Equally staying aware may alert you to a downturn in the market in time for you to look at other options. These could be altering the product, changing the price or producing a variant of the original.

Constant market analysis may well allow you to pick up on an opportunity that your competitors have so far missed. It might be possible to increase supplies to your customers and thereby increase their sales and yours. For example, your customers might say that they would sell more if they have them in stock as opposed to ordering and waiting two days for them. You would then be able to react to this and source the funds to make this possible. Good marketing would also tie your customers in, maybe even requiring an upfront contribution to assist with this.

If you are unable to adapt and change as the needs of your market change you will stagnate and fail.

Chapter 7: Laying foundations for the future

This goes hand in hand with the creation of the business plan and the strategy. You will need to be focused on the daily tasks and your market share. However this is also an important time to lay a foundation for the future.

The personnel you employ now will hopefully be the ones that stay with you whilst the company grows. It is important that you pick people who are either already good in their specific area or have the potential to be. Of equal importance is that these people believe and share in the same vision of the company as you do, that they too want the company to be successful and grow year on year. You will need to be able to get along with the key personnel and it is especially important to ensure the lines of communication between you are always open. Financial rewards will assist in the retention of staff but appreciated staff will stay with you and perform better.

Whilst it is not always possible for a start up to have the capital or time spare to invest in training staff it is a useful tool in staff retention and loyalty. This can be particularly relevant if you are trading in a niche market with limited other opportunities. However you look at creating the foundations of your business looking after your staff is a cornerstone to achieving this.

Customers – the foundation of any business. Without these there is no business. The business plan and strategy have identified, targeted and hopefully gained you your first customers. Retention is now the name of the game. Every transaction with a customer should exceed their expectations. Your company should almost be taken for granted by them because of the quality and reliability of your product. No customer will change suppliers if they are one hundred percent happy with what they are currently getting. Unfortunately it is inevitable that there will be an issue at some point with the supply or the quality of a particular batch or maybe even the service in general. This is the test that, if handled correctly, will ensure the customer stays with you for a lifetime. It is vital that the lines of communication are open and you discuss this issue and possible solutions with them. You will need to come to a solution that both parties can be happy with. More importantly the approach to this will be remembered by your customer. If you are sympathetic and honest in your dealings they will not only remain as your customer you will have increased your reputation and potentially your market share.

Finally an important part of strong foundations is to be prepared to let go. As the company grows it will simply not be possible for you to monitor and control every aspect. As mentioned above it is important from the start to hire people who have a vested interest in the company and who will perform their role in the company as well, if not better than you would. Of equal importance are the procedures you have laid out. You will need to be happy that the daily task lists ensure everything that needs to be completed is. You will then need to be comfortable that there are enough checks in place to ensure the people doing these jobs are doing them properly. Much of this is about giving ownership to those involved in each of the process. Once you are confident that the day to day running of the company is being completed properly and is in good hands you will be free to look to the future. A large part of a good foundation is ensuring you have the time to consolidate your current position and develop ideas for the future. If you are unable to plan ahead (and update your business plan and strategies) you will falter and at best stagnate in the market, quite possibly you will start to lose market share.

Chapter 8: Conclusion

It should now be obvious that the business plan is essential to creating a solid foundation for your company, the strategy is essential for the day to day survival and future growth. The two must go hand in hand for any company to be a success. It should now be fairly obvious that all businesses require them.

It may feel like a mammoth task to prepare the business plan but as you should have seen it is useful in many ways. Writing the plan is time consuming, time that could have been spent starting the business or doing something. However, the business plan is essential to guide the business and the time spent on it is well rewarded further down the line. A plan will ensure that every minute or spare second available is usefully used to improve the business.

The plan will enable you to make informed decisions when choosing the best way forward and for help in tax planning. Allocating funds ready for the tax man should avoid any significant nasty issues. It is always useful to build a small slush fund to ensure you are prepared for any surprises.

A business plan will allow you to evaluate and monitor the day to day running of your new venture and will ensure that the business is moving in the right direction. It relates a lot of information in a few short pages and this information can prove useful at any point in the businesses

It can be a very useful to relist your goals, ambitions and targets at the beginning of each month. This allows you the opportunity to evaluate them, confirm that you are either on track or that you are drifting away from your plan. If this is the case it will be time to adjust the plan or your approach depending on which way is the best way forwards. This also serves to keep you and the staff motivated. You are all working towards a common goal which will make everyone's life better.

This eBook should have assisted you with the preparation of your business plan and allowed you to start a business knowing that you have the basic information at your fingertips and the filing completed. There are many resources available on the internet and it is advisable to utilize as many of them as possible. It is highly unlikely that you can have too much information. Every piece of advice must be assessed for its relevance and helpfulness. Do not be afraid to say it is of no benefit to you.

As you will have seen the key to making the business work is adaptability and flexibility. The economic environment is constantly changing and the plan will need to be updated regularly to ensure it reflects where you are and where you are going.

An important issue which has not been mentioned is the registration of your business. Once you have decided the correct type of business for your needs it will be important to register it as soon as possible. Without registering your business you may find yourself struggling to get merchant accounts or correctly headed paper – all of which aid the professional appearance of your company.

Remember, there is no right or wrong way to write a business plan or to run a business. What works for one will not work for another. Plan as much as you can, research and create strategies but don't forget to do it, give your business venture a chance!